Of Life & Love
"My Journey"

Of Life & Love "My Journey"

Copyright © 2010 Matthew A. Parker

All rights reserved. No portion of this book may be reproduced, stored in a retrieval system, or transmitted in any form or by any means—electronic, mechanical, photocopy, recording, scanning, or any other—except for brief quotations in critical reviews or articles, without prior written permission of the author.

Acknowledgements

This book has been a short work for a long time. I would like to thank the most high, God. Without HIM nothing is possible. I would like to thank every impressionable person who has helped me into the shape of a man that I stand before you as today. To my family I love you all. Good moments, to hardships during those hard times, thank you.

Thank you to each sister, brother, and all my parents because it truly took a village to raise this child. To my mother, Eva Parker, only you have shown me that hard work truly pays off. I could never repay for the sacrifices you made, so your children can have a chance in this world. For my teachers, students, and classmates in the school of life, let us work hard and play harder. For any woman who has left traces of footprints in my heart, thank you. Love is love...

P.S. - A special thank you to her, she knows who she is.

"I am only me, perfectly imperfect, with all the potential and good intentions and anything but average."

Journey

A thousand mile journey begins with just one step
But my steps are fading can't foresee my past the images are negating
The everyday struggle we've been faced with
Wishing I could drift but I can barely float, being pulled under by a lead anchor
But I can barely tread water
And I want to charge it to my upbringing and culture
Tired of passing the blame, no longer will I walk in shame
Taken the beaten path has left me trapped and hurting
No growth but my bones are still spurting
Fighting to not see closed curtains
Man of his word, living on the curve
Played in the streets but never rashed by the curb
But my inner desires to fly like a bird rise like a phoenix
But humble myself to my savior Christ Jesus
Who carries my troubles when I can barely walk
Each step lifting my spirit as I unfold ready to talk
No one asks me to but I speak to all souls
Not the destination but walking that path is the goal
A thousand mile journey has to begin with just one step
I'm the only one in my shoes to decide what's next

A Fire Inside

If you go gentle into the good night
It's like a man has no reason to fight
For life not saying it out of spite
But if you want to die then why live
The point of existence is to give
Not give in, not wasting what you were given
Potential and talents, you must imagine the if's
Why live shy if you're dying inside
Cautious and careful but rather be fearful
Brave men don't heed to this earful
If they ignore it with their ignorant ways
Then this cycle will shorten their days
Like a sailor saluting his last waves
As the flag goes opposite of the raise
You can go quietly or in a roaring blaze
Like a old man bragging about his glory days
Like a young man seizing the moment
Or a good woman getting it whenever she wants it
So don't front it, or defy it
You should redefine it
If darkness falls try to relight it
When it all fails don't start a tall tale
Be bright enough to out burn a fire in hell
Take what is said and use it well
It's a process going quietly is thoughtless
Think of doing more not getting less
Don't cower when it gets tough you take the side way out
Your actions should move people not fill their doubts
So don't go into the good night on a silent ride
If you do your fire may have never been burning inside

A Worker's Struggle

It's always hard staying on my daily grind
Big man, working two jobs just to stay alive
Keeping my head up, working always gives me pride
Keep my hands dirty and sweat in my brow
Cause that's the only way
I've known to make my dollar
cant sleep long all I know is awkward silence
I work this hard so the next generation won't have to try this
so it can't be denied this feeling of escape that burns deep on my inside
Got to stay and work agreeing with my foolish pride
looking out the window at freedom
damn I wish I was on the other side
I work so hard so my lineage understands
What is it the value of a cent
Continue push the dimes
Working up all that overtime
Hoping that my hard work
Truly ends up paying off
And eventually I release myself
From the shackles of this slavery
And find something suitable escape as a laboring emperor
cursed by years of poverty
but still I rise prince among good
king above great
the cause of my will is the dissatisfaction of being a common field hand
never on my knees I take to both feet to stand
rejuvenated when I look into my daughters eyes
it is always I can never just I try
living to do better not just to survive
expanding my horizons while I work to stay alive
Knowing the future is not set on stone
I keep on reaching out to that my future goal
Hoping the hands will be softer as time unfolds
For my children's fate is also my own
In time they will see the greatness they want to be in me
But for now my hustle is where I gots to be

Living paycheck to paycheck for the time being
All this labor, pains and struggle
So the future is ahead of its past ancestry
when they don't have to sacrifice they think of me
work harder than I do knowing their best is #1
and provide as I have for their generations of daughters & sons

Hard Work Is My Hustle

If you can't work hard you can't hustle
Cuz hustling takes a lot of hard work
And hard work is the ultimate hustle
So if you b.s. will walk not just talk then I've got to burst your bubble
My hard work is hustle
My grind is 9 to 5 moving never slacking on mine
not the rat race but I can step with a quick pace
and the devilish smirk to compliment the smooth poker face
hustlers' eyes always darting and dancing but most have no clue
that my mind is running the odds of chances, that my goal is to out-hustle you
cuz you can't work harder than I work, my work is my hustle, my hustle is my pride, my pride is the reason my spirit of hard work doesn't die
I see most hustles as a way of means
whether its women of the nights moving, or a soldiers fulfilling dreams
but my hustle is for me not the next man
he could never walk in my shoes or follow thru my plans
can't move forward too busy looking behind
my hard work is me so I got a piece of mind
but don't sleep I can easily walk with a piece a nine
but more of a gentleman in public but its whatever in private
closed lips don't get kissed
cool demeanor so I've never been dissed
my hustle factor starts the chain reactor working in over-drive
I will stop anything that tries to reach over mine
cuz you can't work harder than I work, my work is my hustle, my hustle is my pride, my pride is the reason my spirit of hard work doesn't die
nobody is going to undermine my ego
I move myself, next is my people, don't you know I will see you
My hard work makes your hustle see through
you think what I know my hard work keeps my hustle humble so that I reap what I sow
My hustle is hard work within limitless lines

Hard work is a hustle that takes patience and time
Hustle to keep up
hard work to maintain
Hustle to be number # 1
cuz hard work + hustle is how I'm a gain
cuz you can't work harder than I work, my work is my hustle, my hustle is my pride, my pride is the reason my spirit of hard work doesn't die

"Balance the power struggle of good and evil, internally and externally…"

Facing Myself

Do I see a man or a monster?
Do I see two sides of the same coin?
Looking at my extremities
The stocky build and slender smile
Looks to kill from a devilish hood child
Eyes ready that see through all with amused thoughts
Hands tough from a hard days work
But if you look deep in me you can understand my worth
Staring back at my reflection
I struggle with contempt and deception
Was born with broad shoulders to carry the weight of the world
But a compassionate demeanor that sees the innocence of every little boy and girl
I behold eyes that forgive in this reflection as I search for my own soul
Being my own man in this life has taken its toll
Each look in the mirror smiles, or frowns back
Tears of pain or joy temporarily mar this same face
Just another reflection of self as I look in the same place
Facing myself

Confused Fears

Things done changed
The last days I've been enraged
But days have been years
Can't cope pride won't let me shed tears
Grown now seen so much I have no fears
Or do I?
Let me Go back and see
All those things that have scarred or scared me:
Lost so much don't know how to gain
If it weren't for my family I couldn't maintain
Or stay starving hungry for the world
But extra weight on my back
Chased by fiends in hallways smoking on crack
Part of my past is plagued
I wish I were killed by HIV/AIDS
Or some other syndrome
Not fortunate enough to have a happy home
Been through some shit still with no plan
No father around teaching me to be a man
Stand on my own two
Had mom's but what could she do
Couldn't prepare me for what I'd go through
I will tell all I love my mother no matter what happened I won't choose another
Some times I felt smothered but you had my back and took my cover
For that I am grateful
Pushing me and my success when your days are so painful
When you pain I hurt you seeded me
That's more than any other woman's worth
But now I gotta make it past my past
Present myself in the present
Start to look in the mirror without resentment
And then only then survive for my future
Look near and far
For whom ever can teach me to reach for the stars
But I can't, its like I settle for failure or am I scared of success
Cause its not in my reach or put in my tense

Why can't I try my best
Work hard, think harder, try hardest
Maybe things done changed
I'm so enraged by my past days fearing if their my last days
But days have been years
So now to sum it all up
No father figure just a man that busted a nut
Bearing witness to drugs
Schooling dropped came in fell out
Not gangster but still acts of a thug
No real jail time just struggling not to fail mine
Treated people like trash because I never really knew how to love
Seeded up now cuz I was probably too high to pay attention to using a glove
Public figure that privately cries
Still want to crawl up in the darkest corner and cry
Push away any one that tries to come near
Another incomplete cycle of a confused man's fears

"I am a great mind, a tempted body, a kind heart and a confused soul. I am human."

Losing

I hate losing to gain
I feel suffering to all ends
so I no longer feel pain
If pain is my comfort then joy has left me
abandoned like a bastard child
alone with pain in my spirit
wish you were here to help me bear with it
the fight inside starts to go wild
l wish l didn't have to settle
or feelings would begin to mettle
and not just melt
away….
away from losing I'm ready to gain
or regain self
I feel suffering to all ends
wishing to make amends
distance has made things estranged
no gain, I hate losing
this is not of my choosing
the last time is like replaying the first
time never stood still but the pain still hurts
have yet to bury my sorrow in the earth
scorch my pain into ashes till it blows away into the wind
until my tears stop raining on my own demise
losing to gain is not smart but the experience makes me wise
I hate losing

Time To Man Up

damn...
so hard to man up
don't come empty handed when it's time to man up
its easy to be so tired, easy to lose focus, not hard to give up
Quit. see what you don't do, abandoning responsibility
no reckoning for your liability, lacking your own stability
no reason to be an absent father, a missing son, or a tardy brother,
or a delinquent friend
time to man up
no man down, no sad frown, stop listening to put downs build up
let go of the sinking ship so much pressure from your peers you can't get drowned
time to reap what you sow, not get it for the low
so what your process is slow, your progress slower
you don't get up and go, adversity is basking in the luminous glow
man up times are hard but so are you
find your fit in the world and make do
push, pull, train, and trust
make sure you have more than a dying wish
because its time to man up

Selfishly Selfless

selfish or selfless
do what is right for others or do what is the right time for you
selfish
to be the best or to be compassionate
selfless
trying to do the most good or get it done because its
understood
selfish
to serve or to slave, or to go unappreciated each and every day
selfless
follow my own burning desire or help by stepping thru those
incorrigible fires
selfish or selfless
when am I selfish how am I selfless
not me to stop me as I share we all strive
if we lose commitment to self then apart of me dies
not greed or glutton but we need more
if I am selfish then we all are selflessly reaping no rewards
now is that...
selfless or selfish

"Do more, be better, and put yourself first. Not selfishly, just righteously."

Just My Thoughts

a thought is present, a thought is near
sometimes only the questions are clear
at least in my life there aren't always answers
because life is the answer in itself
there are so few people with fame and wealth
how do I feel?
some have luxury while I remember when there wasn't always a meal
I don't look to them with admiration and envy
I learn about the things in life that that keep your heart filled and plenty
plenty of good feelings and free will
but my next thought is my desires and goals aren't filled
no more are the dreams of being a famous rapper or actor
but my plight may have me one day speaking God's rapture
listening to what's inside of you
just my thoughts of right or wrong things to do
thinking of each life that is pick or choose
all for nothing trying not to lose
use my mind through kind pure thoughts
use something else and probably be caught
I know right away to give all I got
it all had to start with just my thoughts...

"A moment of embarrassment can become a lifetime of humility."

Too Late

Thinking about thinking until you can't think
A lifetime passes for every moment you blink
A blank stare into an oblivion of cares, feelings, and emotions
That are encroaching on the substance of the word "if"
If I could, if you would, if it did
While thinking about thinking until you can't think
I realize to move forward I have to get past the brink
The brink of gonna's, have to's, and the incomplete try
Because if I never do then life will keep passing me by
A day late, a dollar short, off task, waiting to be next
Worrying about others but failing to protect my own neck
Never slow don't give in, take control of your own fate
Live life full now cause it can never be too late...

Is She

Is she...
Is she mine,
My question that is posed at this moment in time
Divine and eloquent,
Style and swag that is unmatched
Is she mine,
I want her to be my catch
Watch her close
Touch her, closer
Inhale her, just because she is...
She is greatness
If she gives me the faintest of hints
I would steal cupid's arrows and never miss
We both could be falling and never hit
Her outs are my ins
As we consume in our thoughts that are shared
My out will join her in
and we'd ride that wave of bliss
Now it's not just she or me, its "we"
Is she, the other half of me?
Now I'm wishing it to be
Just hope she doesn't hurt me
I want her nurture, her strength, and honesty
Can she carry me
Carry my love, my care
Allow me to rescue her from any moments despair
I want her, but does she care
Not to be single is she ready to pair
Am I selfishly thinking, because I don't want to share....
Is she ready to be there
Is she...
Is she mine?

Can He...

Can he be mine? Will he be Mine, is the Question she is posing at this time..
Can he be the one to win my heart, and I give it without guarding it anymore?
Can he be the one to console me, support me, love me, hold me, comfort me and even lead me all in One?
Can he be the one to erase the images I have of men being users, bad liars and flat out Dogs?
Can he be the one to provide me with that permanent glow of pure happiness and oneness with a like spirited person?
Can he be my equal as well as my biggest supporter?
Are these just questions I have running through my head, or do these answers lay somewhere in his heart?
Together, can we combine two souls and make them one?
Filling each other with that missing piece we couldn't find in any other one
Together, can we produce that love that so many people lack seeing on a daily basis?
Together, can we produce children that will mirror US and the love we share in our home?
You may wonder Is She, but in my heart I know he can and will be all I need, In time...
Though time stands still for No woman or man, at this particular moment, I applaud time for being just right for Us...

Love is Love

My Challenge

I remember the first time we spoke
I couldn't remember her name but then there's that frog in my throat
But I wanted to speak informally about us becoming formal
Becoming formal us, we's, they's, and their's but She tossed those thoughts into the wind then it blew thru the air
Then I realized that is was her heart that I sought to win
Time moved fast but I did not
Before I knew it, it was almost too late to talk
Just by chance I saw her look my way
I thought I was cool, cheesing, then come with the same ol' corny line,
"Hey Ms., how you doing today?"
She challenged my look and shot down my line by spitting back,
"Before you spoke, I was doing just fine"
Unraveled I decided to stay persistent
Cuz I knew I could get her if I did more than wished it
A few months have passed as this "thing" would go back and forth
Now there were smiles and cute hello's instead of smart remarks and clever retorts
I noticed her quiet strength when I'd closely admire her
I wanted to warm that cold in her heart with my inside fire
But I can't lie that led me to be inspired by her
Cuz she is my challenge
I told her I desired her
Cuz she is my challenge
But she wouldn't have it
Cuz she is my challenge
She was pretty much saying tricks are for kids and she was never a rabbit
Even still, our bond was becoming close, our time was consumed with sharing our passion of what we can do.
We'd vent, we'd debate, it was always love never was there any hate
Through that there was a chance, almost a real date
But we missed

Naw, I missed
Now my miss was his gain
So now my miss is like his Mrs.
We still try to motivate and match
I'm still hoping that she'll become my catch
But my ego won't allow My challenge to have bested me where I still lack
She didn't mean to do that
She is my challenge
But my challenge wasn't really a challenge
She just showed me things I wasn't ready to see
I hope that she sees that I found in pursuing her I found the challenge in me

"It's all about the perfect moment. When eyes connect, a warm embrace, it feels like the worlds going a million miles a moment, but the time is standing still while you hold her... A perfect fit, you both lean forward for that magic to take place... and... and.. damn alarm clock wakes you up!!"

Will We

Not a moment's still as we rise to the occasion
Still I fight to be what she needs
Will We
Forget what is said, follow or know when to be led
No anticipating, every moment in her presence has my heartbeat reach new heights
She is more than a new high but the love is so good I feel like Im floating on every cloud in the sky
Will We
Be as comfortable and match like a favorite pair of shoes,
She is my diamond that's never rough
To her I am more than special enough
Never a comparison, the others were just fool's gold
With her by my side we will reach our true goals
"Is She" was my question
"Can He" was her response
"Will We"
Is what's left for the remaining thoughts
Of where it is, what it will be, and how to...
Never too late I hope, or can it be too late too soon
Unique may come once a day so that's a year's worth of reasons to see
"Is She" and "Can He" become "They Do" instead of just "Will We"

My Passion

my passion is...
smiling at the thought of you moving to the beat of the drum
no music just the smooth clicks and clacks and soft hum
as I think of the music that plays thru my mind as you walk in it
rose petal soft the scent of your essence is subtle yet sweet
I can devise several ways to take advantage of you in my sights
you being down solidifies my vantage point, right
my passion is...
the butterflies in my stomach flicker
our energies bond as our bodies come nearer
how do I explain this euphoria that I feel that can't be contained
You have me in smiles at the mere mention of your name
I yearn for the moment that you are near
but I don't want us to part that's a true fear
but my passion is...
promoting feelings that are shedding like true tears
emotions that erupt like celebrations of new year's
our desires ignite fiery passion that is quite clear
that is what
my passion is...

...Addicted...

I'm addicted...
I'm addicted to you...
I'm addicted to you like a fiend
I feel like this natural high is so euphoric that I want everyone to have a try
at first I was so nervous that beads of sweat formed at the slope of my forehead, slowly touched the dent of my brow, gliding down the side of my cheek, and falls off my chin as droplets of knowledge hit the ground
as these thoughts retrace I yearn for more when your around
call me a fiend baby
as I hope, I wish, and I dream baby
to find you again not just my pusher but like a close friend
you're a lovely joy when I found you like when a painter finds his passion as his brush first strokes a canvas
or am I just another fool
fooled into believing that it's okay to drift off as this potion draws its effect
that pulls me in different directions
part forces me to acknowledge the power and influence it holds over my soul
the other part pushes me to see myself for what it is
pushes me to face those fears fight those tears
accept being admired ignore the undesired
but I yearn for it though I hate it at the same time
You have me relive all those feelings, your my word and my scribe
You're my definition of "...To Be..."
I see you in my veins that my blood flows through
to learn more of me I had to get to know you
travel thru my moving lips and fingertips
and maneuver as you are in my grasp
my mind ponders, the pen becomes a wand
on paper magical words appear so I got more powers with you than those 3 chicks on Charmed
I'm addicted...
I'm addicted to you...
you're my outlet, my inlet, a specialty that many can have but I know that we fit
you're my poetry gift, my haiku, my love story, my naughty

thoughts,
my acoustic definitions of things I thought nobody ever got
you're my spoken word piece that I can go and on forever about
cuz God knows I can talk on and on forever about whatever
from you I could never withdraw
but I could always O.D.
your my poetry that I'm addicted to
I'm like a true fiend, you could be right there and I'd still be missing you
every thought of a rhyming word is like sniffing a line,
every metaphor for life is like taking two injections at a time
to not feel you is like going to Betty Ford and be away from you
I'm addicted...
call me that fiend
cuz when things get tough you're what I need
I'm addicted to you...
cuz I'm addicted to you...

"People are like onions, at first they seem plain as we peel back the layers and go deeper, the beauty or the smell can make us all cry."

When You're Not In It

what is love?
who thought of it?
I'm not sure who did, but I'm hatefully thankful for it
the thing is, who the hell cares
why should it matter who should be in a relationship to share
and share for what?
there's no real point, its like saying I do without the ring to anoint.
put a ring on it? girl please. once I do then you don't wanna get on your hands and knees
pain, suffering, and heartache. who needs it? not I.
if I ever see love I might just run and hide.
naw, I don't need that. love will keep you sore, sorry, whinny, and crying
after all that you even get the bill for dining.
not for 1, but for 2.
can't forget the one who smiles and says they love you in between chews
I say if that love is real, she won't ask to go out, you can come home to a hot cooked meal
and she won't get mad she cleaned between the mattress and found the porno mag
but she stay complaining even tho when u top some nights u know she be faking
good luck to bad it may not have worked out
instead of never falling in love, you may never figure it out

What Could Have Been

lust, passion, feelings, and realization
these are the things attract people together
though the reasons are unclear
and what you thought was uncertainty was really your hidden fears
after long amounts of time sense was finally made
my emotions are about to blow up like exploding grenades
thinking about that one time as it replays in my mind
everything feels like its changing but why is my heart in rewind
its like I build myself up for disappointment
blessing my presence with you was my prayers' request without fulfilled anointment
when I think everything's right and just in place
I knew nothing was happening because she couldn't look me in the face
when all the talk that took place over many moonless skies
it just brings back all those heartfelt pains from that night
was it because of the past that we're at a crossroads contemplation
maybe one day I can let go of the hurt and emotional defecation
I can't help but feel like I'm over thinking what should have been
Deep down we both know what could've been

"The quest for romance, is it rivalry or ritual to fight for love?"

Old Love/ New Love

It wasn't supposed to be like this
but I don't want to lose either him
not sure that my man will stay but I was angered so I made him a angry man
then I saw another man,
who became my other man, but that wasn't my plan
It sort of just happened
he made me feel magic
when he touched me it tingled,
plus when we met he said it was okay that I wasn't single
so I enjoy our time spent cause that's what I needed
damn shame my man still don't even see it
sometimes I wish he could see, catch me
so I can be rid of these lies
but....
I like to have my cake and eat it too!
if either one cared they would ask more than "what can he do?"
I used to love it when he'd steal me away from the world
now my other man is calling me his "special girl"
my man said he will decide when its over
I know that ish is wrong
but this ain't another sad love song
Plus I told him Im bout ready to do me
my man said he would put me in the grave before my body got cold
if I ever thought about being that bold
so....
I am a woman scorned
no
I'm just getting what I want cuz I stopped settling for no
my man worries about giving in so easily
that I got the other man, cause he always pleases me
sometimes its so hard to choose which one is really for me
the strong, boring provider, or the one not too proud to get on his hands and knees
my old love, fits me like an old glove
I know my heart is torn cuz this old love is worn

while new love is astounding
just his presence is alone, quickens my heart pounding
but its pure desire, no control
that's why I don't know which love to let go...
what's next?

All The Women

he arises from his bed of lies
the latest victim still in her motionless slumber
in his thoughts he recalls last night's cries
"Ooh baby, yes daddy, give me more"
he's heard it so many times now he just gets bored
once he learned how to have his way
they'd all give him what he wants just to be his if only for a day
his reckless abandon, nonchalant demeanor, and sensitive touch
he tells each her what she wants to hear until he gets to nut
each one thinks it's just her but they know the truth by and by
he loves them all that's why he doesn't have to lie
he says don't ask me, I won't tell you"
He omits, he relishes in its significance
that is becoming more significant
as he professes his love to all the women, each her
fascinated by her curves, loving her scents
he feels each her is heavenly sent
each body he lays down he wants to conquer
they give his kingship the ability to rule their thrones
all the women that have touched his bed and forgot about their happy homes
his secrets, their lies, through the sheets and between all thighs
each on different emotional highs
he smiles as they cry
all the women's faces he sees riding him from atop to when he slides from behind
arrays of hues and shades, unique colors and creams
only in the moment of bliss do they stand out thru hollers and screams
all the women

"My most prized possession is your girlfriend's heart."

Being The Other Man

being a man is hard but being her other man is...
special
it takes so much to get on this level
to understand what it takes
to stay patient without haste
get all her wants no worries about her needs
I know when she says what to do I always leave her pleased
Im known to stretch her walls of inhibition
circumstance affords us to play in multiple positions
cuz I am her muse like she is my model
pouring on those compliments
that she shaped like an hour glass or a coke bottle
but I keep her in place while staying in mine
not once do I mention how's the "first" guy
he ain't handling his so why should I pry
to tell the truth I don't even know their names
and hope they wont figure out mines
cuz when he finds plumber in her book,
it means I'm mentally, physically, and emotionally cleaning her pipes
reminiscent of the sheer bliss
that she gets from me with a sealed kiss
don't be fooled, I know there's rules to this
feelings are okay cuz I got mine in check
no rookie moves, I'm a seasoned vet
for every move there could be a consequence
I stay with a upper hand that is my confidence
its a hard line to walk
to know so all the secrets that can't be talked
I know her truths and she understands
at the end of the day I'm just being her other man

Do Me A Favor (It's Over)

Its over
I don't know how to thank her
for showing her true colors
see, I was definitely distracted whenever we were in close proximity
wool was over my eyes while everyone saw what she did to me
never a foolish man, just too filled with pride
so when lies came to surface, l would help them hide
couldn't put my foot down, didn't ever talk tough
l figured the storm would past thru if l just love her enough
but l also see now that l can't do this all on my own
can't find her for days and she ain't answering the phone
she says she wish l were better or different
no matter what l try she just becomes more and more distant
Its over
so now l don't want to fix it
to me, this is it!
no more playing me like l'm a dog chasing a biscuit
l know who he is and his is coming too
I can tell when he comes through
so you can stop lying about wearing his
scent cuz that burberry cologne don't belong to you
sad, your thinking about him while you were out with me
spare me the bullshit tell the truth outta love not
lie outta sympathy
you say you're not a player but cards are dealt and all can see your hand
l see that fool playing the role of being 'the other man'
but trust the 80/20 rule is always true
that 80 from me is now all gone
hope that 20 you got caught creeping with won't leave you alone
now that l got outta my heart what l want to say
do me a favor, and stay the hell away
Its over

"Sex and Love: Both, sometimes, come too quick and when it's gone it'll have you feeling like you wish you can have it all over again."

The High Note That Is Me

Im the beat of the bass
its the sound of the snares
the drums that go pow, bam, boom
oh yes that was heard by me too
notice the blaring horns
becoming louder than the screams of a woman scorned
listen closely no sound but the music that is me
well it still plays on
pushing for higher standards like rehearsals of repetition
I can never stop until I get it
wont give up cuz only losers deserve quitting
as I flash my smile of ivory keys
you can understand my winning please
building up the momentum
timing is huger than the pendulum
climbing up the climatic peak
so you can understand the high note that is me
and why music is my escape route and a life long journey
between bars of spirit
and lyrics of hope
the chorus is the summary of this life evoked
put on the front line
choosing is like picking a bass guitar over trombone
both sound nice, feel right,
play different but if you do it wrong they'll never play right
so you must practice like you play
this music is my sway
it can keep you up all night
or a beginning and ending to a lovers' fight
closure is now meant for this closer
the high note that is me
for I am the composer...

Sweet Motion

look at that sweet motion
Your curves move as smooth as waves in the ocean
Movement as perfect as a flawless crystal
I can't sit here and imagine
I see that we're a lot alike and feel we are matching
I feel like you're the jackpot but only I should cash in
Not just trying to get you "In"
But more of a including
Include the sexual, mental, and even a little lyrical
If we go any further we can relate to our conceptual
Let you sweet motion rise while I climb my tongue across your peaks
Turn over on your stomach
Slide all around while my lips dance on your sweet motioning cheeks
Cuz I know how much we both want it
Roll those full hips, and arch your back
Ready the position, I push into your engine with my love train piston
Your mouth slightly agape as you whisper
We move in rhythm like a synchronized unison
No words are needed because our bodies are listening
I give your sweet motion a slap of motivation
You bite my neck giving me renewed sensations
Beads of love moisture start to coat our bodies
You tell me to apologize for beating it up but I won't say sorry
Then things get starry, you buck hard pushing while I pull
If I let go right now I'd be a damn fool
I lean forward putting my all in
You tell me if I finish the race now then we both don't win
I hold tight keeping back that selfish release seeking a deeper high
You moan and yell all those ecstasy-filled cries
I palm both halves of your world in the grips of my hands
Then lose myself in you like sliding into quick sand
I'm thinking fast moving slow to let you know we are on the same path
I watch you jiggle from side to side as I enjoy your magic

carpet ride
Sweet motion has me in a trance
Then my legs shake your love tunnel starts to funnel I lose control
But I know to finish the ride never let that sweet motion go
I ask if it's time you clench that bottom lip and give a slow wind
It felt like spring as we both rained on the sheets
The sweetest motion was a fulfilling treat

"It may take a village to raise a child, but a man can uplift his people"

My People

From Africa to the deep dark depths of the southern places in this nation
My People
are suffering from 400 years of oppressed sanitation
segregation, prejudice, hatred, slavery
My People
their manipulation of lives was deceptively clever
movement on boats and chains of lies that will never return
befriending when their the enemy that burns
I still can't hate no matter how much deep down inside I try
above all I realized I'm not just black on the outside
My People
we've come to know that we breathe the same air
My People
were set free but we still stayed scared
scarred for life forced into carpet bagging
trained to hurt ourselves for false swaging
put our tails between our legs and run away
not My People,
that's not how we were made
lynching and burnings now we were called names out of spite
keeping us fighting each other and not having equal rights
to live in peace not having to watch over our backs
My People
just like white hoods our black panthers made their own packs
faceless figures too stingy to share what they stack
My people
are or should I say figure heads with hidden agendas
they promise the promise land
then they tell My people we are not misled
but if we believe that then why is our future the past and our present hanging over our heads
My People
no one wants to repeat history so somehow it can be undone
not saying to blame anybody or any man but there's still work for
My people before we say we won
For my people I can't go out like that

No one should walk away and let go of the slack
Instead of just defending My people
Its time for My people to stand united
having each other's backs
For My People
you are, My People
I am, My People
We are all, My People

My Sole-An Ode To Thy Sneaker

there's nothing like your sweet smell
every inhale is like breathing for the first time
when I look at your sole I become mesmerized,
I can only imagine the places we will travel
how we'll stay connected even when that new feeling unravels
I think of the moments that are going to be shared
or all of those jealous eyes from me handling you with care
don't worry or fret cause when I lace you we both are snapping necks
what is that you might ask
why is my ex pair put in the trash
all I have to say is that the past is the past
don't worry about them that's why they're my last
right now you are my fave
I bought you but your worth much more than what I paid
to me your more than the latest fad
and if the next person tries to step on you we both will kick their a$$
cuz I feel you from the inside you make me feel like I'm floating on air
and don't worry its not cheating if I buy another pair
its just I don't want that feeling to ever go away
I dream about how good you'll look when I get dressed every day
summer, spring, fall, or winter's cold
I love you always cuz your my sole

"It all takes time, with an open heart and an open mind."

Free

I want to be free
I want my expressions to resemble
creative styles of abstract independent rhythm
that flows like a jazz session with the synchronization of the boston pops orchestra
my life is disorganized as a mosh pit at a rock show
I yearn for the synergy like the fusion of a classical masterpiece and hip hop quotable
or a freestyle flow like punch lines, high pitch adlibs with the riffs of samples of R'n'B greats but my life holds on to things like a heavy load that I carry on with ignoring that its too heavy for my arms to lift
but I press on because the bag that is a heavy load contains the good and the bad
I learn to smile through life's pleasures and pains not staying sad
even though I'd rather grimace and grind my teeth
my blessings are lessons that I could never teach
I still search for this freedom
I know I am the ruling in my kingdom
cause, effect, timing, circumstance, and mostly God keep me free
by gifting me with a heavy load of treasures and adversities I will always be
so I continue to push through
so I fight the pain that strikes like hearing mary j. cry
or hearing repeated hip hop artist kill their communities by telling lies
the gospel hymns play in my head like a Sunday morning at the front pew
every time things in my life don't make sense like a drunken country tune
I can drop to my knees at nite and pray under the moon
I know through God's voice in me all things can be
and only through him I can truly be free

To My Readers

I figured out that life is never easy. Love makes it even tougher. When you see something or someone you want, don't be afraid to go for it. Having no regrets is easy, living is daily and attaining your dreams is where the fun and hard work begins…

~Matthew A. Parker